Charles C Somerville

A

Africa

Protected by desert on both sides and mountains to the south, Egypt, in north-east Africa, grew along the banks of the Nile to become the most developed civilization in the ancient world.

Ancient Egypt

Ancient Egypt was the first proper nation in history, with its defined boundary, its common culture and with a pharaoh in charge who made all the rules (and you didn't argue with the pharaoh!). It proved to be a successful and prosperous system and that's why it survived for more than 3,000 years.

As well as being part of a strong nation, Egyptians were ingenious and understood science and mathematics. This allowed them to build great temples and pyramids. They were also artistic and created paintings, sculptures and jewellery to worship the sun god Ra and a few hundred other gods for good measure.

The Egyptians believed in life after death, so devoted a fair amount of time and energy to making sure they'd be around to enjoy a better life when they were dead.

While life may have been quite different 5,000 years ago, the Egyptian people wouldn't have been any different from you and me.

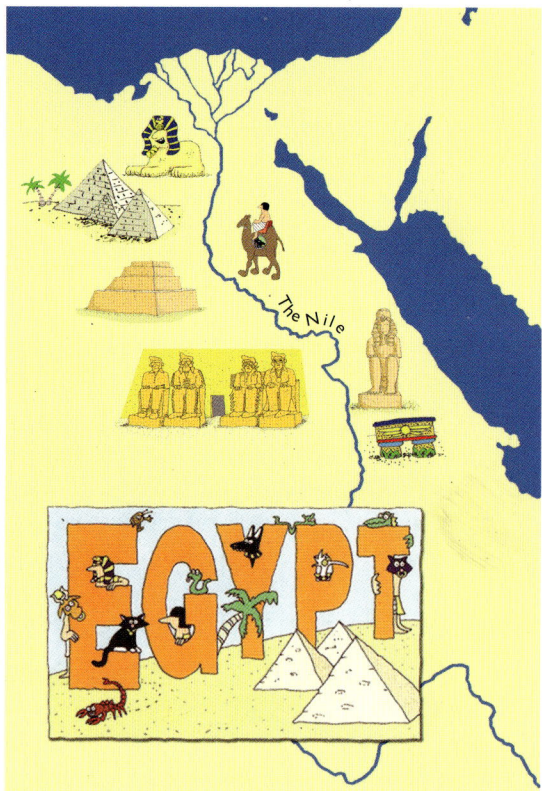

Archaeology

Much of what we know about Ancient Egypt is through the study of objects, which archaeologists have found buried in the desert. Egypt's hot, dry climate means that much is preserved, including papyrus (paper) records. Careful where you dig though – there may be scorpions about!

Afterlife

Egyptians believed in a wonderful place called the "Afterlife" – often described as a "field of reeds". It consisted of lush farmland and well-watered orchards and gardens, providing plentiful harvests and peace and tranquillity. This was a perfect world where you would live forever, but it took more than dying to get there. First your body had to be mummified to preserve it and then you had to pass through the terrifying underworld.

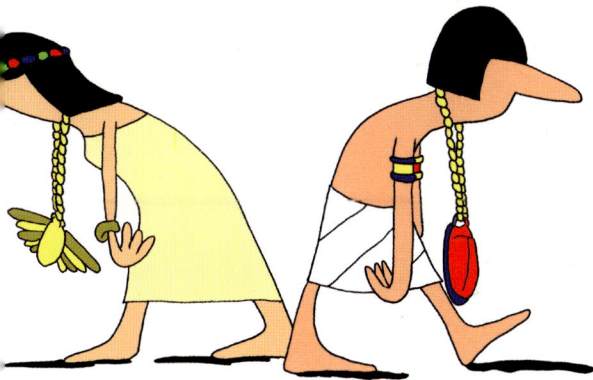

Amulets

An amulet was a lucky charm worn by Egyptians to ward off evil. Some were shaped like scarabs (a type of beetle thought to be divine), while others featured religious symbols, such as winged disks and ankhs (a cross with a loop at the top).

Book of the Dead

Everyone in Egypt wanted to end up in the Afterlife, but getting there wasn't easy. Fortunately, you had writings from the "Book of the Dead" in your tomb, which were full of tips, tricks, charms and spells to guide you on your way.

Ba

Picture this funny-looking fellow, called a Ba, with your face on it (you can take or leave the false beard). Egyptians believed this winged creature would fly from your mummified body to be reunited with your Ka (your life force and body double) and form your Akh, which was needed to survive in the Afterlife. It is where the expression "getting your akh together" probably didn't come from.

Beetle

This humble dung beetle (also called a scarab beetle) represented hope and rebirth for Egyptians. They believed it rolled the sun across the sky each day in the same way a beetle rolls a ball of dung across the sand.

C

Crocodiles

Rich nobles kept crocodiles as status symbols in their homes, while priests allowed them to roam freely around temples.

Often the crocs were dressed in jewels – I suppose they would have been called "snappy dressers".

Cartouche

Pharaohs liked their name to stand out, so when they had temples or tombs built, their name was carved into the walls in an oval frame called a "cartouche".

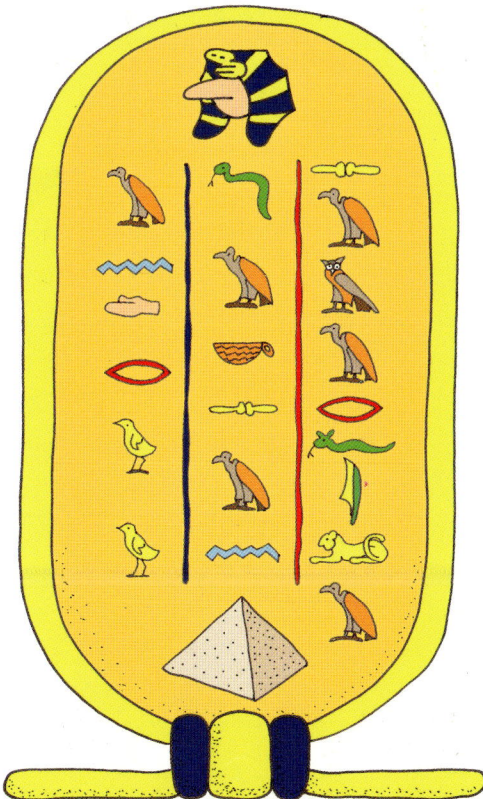

Cats

Incredible! The more I ignore them, the more they treat me like a god.

Egyptians loved animals (they thought they were gods in disguise) and were particularly fond of cats. Other sacred animals included: hawks, ibises, dogs, lions and baboons. Anyone who deliberately killed a sacred animal was put to death. Even accidental killings could be punished.

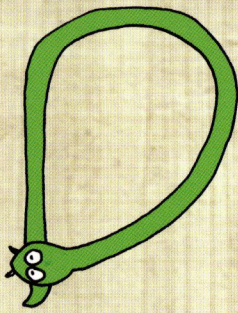

Dynasty

The first known Egyptian king was Menes, who is believed to have brought together the Upper and Lower Kingdoms of Egypt in about 3,000 BC.

To help deal with the huge number of kings who followed Menes, an Egyptian priest and historian called Manetho divided them into 30 ruling families or "dynasties". Manetho compiled his lists of kings about 2,300 years ago from writings on clay tablets and papyrus scrolls, passed down through the centuries.

The last native Egyptian dynasty fell to the Persians in 343 BC (which was named by modern scholars as the 31st dynasty). This ended in 332 BC with the conquest by Alexander the Great from Greece. Rome then invaded in 30 BC and Egypt became just another Roman province (albeit an impressive one).

Eye of Horus

Horus was a falcon and the god of the sky. The pharaoh was believed to be the human incarnation of Horus on earth. The Eye of Horus was a symbol of royal power, good health and protection, and is found in many paintings and carvings, and on amulets.

Egyptology

Egyptology is the study of Ancient Egypt and includes its history, literature, religion, language and art. It goes hand in hand with archaeology and helps us to understand about the Egyptians' everyday life.

Right

Wrong

Everyday life

Life was pretty good for most Egyptians – there was no shortage of food, there was medicine if you were ill and people lived in comfortable homes.

Children and adults had time to enjoy themselves too – they played board games, fished and enjoyed sport. While they probably didn't play golf (which would have presented problems finding the green), they did play a game a bit like hockey.

Flies

Flies were a nuisance in Ancient Egypt and at one time fly-swatters, made from giraffe tails, became all the rage. King Pepi II had his own solution, which the giraffes would have preferred. He ordered his servants to coat themselves in honey to attract the pesky insects – so there were no flies on him.

Feather of Truth

The final test an Egyptian had to face before reaching the Afterlife was the "weighing of the heart". The heart, which was believed to contain all a person's good and bad deeds, was placed on a huge pair of golden scales and weighed by the god Anubis against the "feather of truth". The more bad deeds you'd committed, the heavier your heart would be.

If you'd been good, then you'd be taken to the Afterlife. But if not, and your heart tipped the scales the wrong way, then things wouldn't be so great. Not only would you fail to enter the Afterlife, but your heart would be eaten by Ammut – a demon, with the face of a crocodile and legs of a hippo.

Woof! Sorry, I meant Grrr!

Gods

There were hundreds, if not thousands, of gods in Ancient Egypt. Most were part human, part animal. Some were more popular than others depending on where in Egypt you lived. Pharaohs often favoured certain gods and commanded the priests and people to worship them. Important gods included: Anubis, Osiris, Ra, Bastet, Hathor, Horus, Isis, Nut (real name!), Seth and Geb. Most of them looked really creepy …

All pharaohs were considered to be gods. They built scores of statues of themselves – in case you ever forgot!

When the gods are angry.

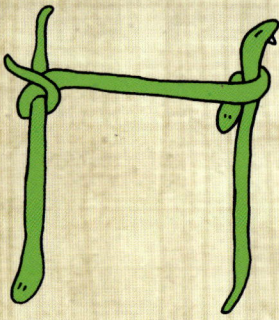

Hieroglyphics

Hieroglyphics was the formal writing of Ancient Egypt. It looked like a secret picture code and was carved into the walls of temples, pyramids and tombs. Unfortunately, nearly 2,000 years after the end of the Ancient Egyptian civilisation, there was no one left who remembered what they meant and so they remained a mystery – at least until the discovery of the Rosetta Stone ...

… In 1799, while Napoleon was trying to take over Europe, he decided northern Africa looked a good bet too. One of his soldiers tripped over a stone tablet outside the port of Rosetta. The Rosetta Stone, as it became known, was inscribed in hieroglyphics as well as running characters and Greek, and so provided the key to unlocking the hieroglyphic alphabet.

It all looks Greek to me!

Hippopotamus

In addition to birds and crocodiles, there were hippos hanging around in the Nile. Although they look friendly, they were actually more dangerous than the crocs, especially for those who liked to indulge in a spot of hippo hunting. Some Egyptologists now think that King Tutankhamen may have met his end while taking part in this popular sport; and King Menes, who ruled Egypt 2,000 years before him, was also said to have been killed by a hippo.

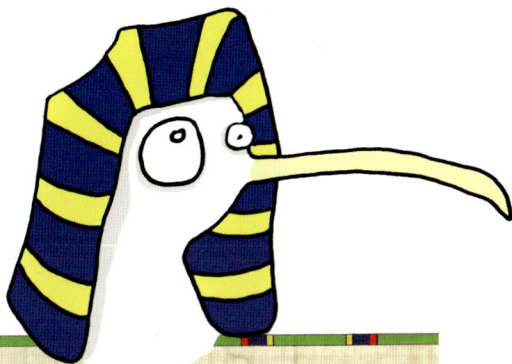

He can't even spell!

Inventions

Egyptians invented many of the things we still use today, such as paper, pens, locks and keys, the flute and, believe it or not, toothpaste (made with ground-up ox hooves).

Next time you're given a pair of woollen socks for Christmas, remember you need to thank the Egyptians for them too – they invented knitting.

Egyptians were the first people to divide the day into 24 hours and used the first shadow clocks (sundials) to tell the time. They also invented the 365-day calendar, an idea they came up with more than 6,000 years ago.

Ibis

An ibis is a stork-like bird, which lives in northern Africa. Egyptians believed it was sacred and even gave one of their gods (Thoth) the head of an ibis. Thoth was the god of writers or scribes (and probably lawyers).

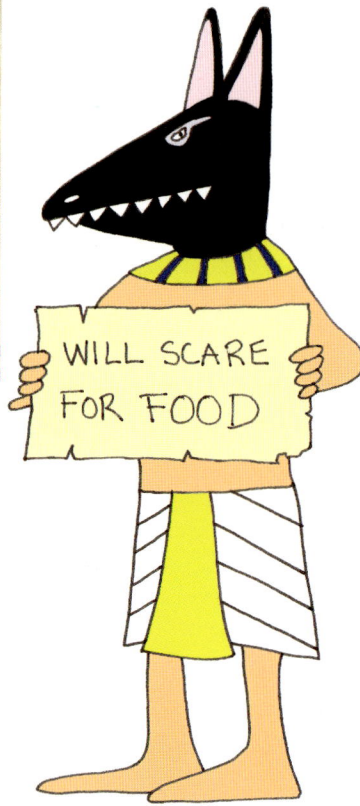

Jackal

One of the creepiest gods was Anubis. He had the head of a jackal (a sort of wild dog) and watched over the dead. Priests sometimes wore a jackal mask to look like the god Anubis.

WILL SCARE FOR FOOD

Jaw-dropping

Part of the Egyptian funeral ceremony involved opening the mouth of the mummy – so it could breathe in the Afterlife.

Jewellery

Jewellery was worn for protection as much as for decoration. It was thought to guard the wearer from mysterious evil forces.

Egyptians made jewellery out of gold and silver, with inlaid semi-precious stones, such as turquoise, amethyst, feldspar and lapiz lazuli. Men wore this type of jewellery as well as women, but only if they were rich and important. The poor wore jewellery made from copper and shells.

Looking good was important to Egyptians. Both men and women wore make-up. The eye-paint was usually green (made from copper) or black (made from lead). As well as giving protection from the sun, Egyptians believed it had magical healing powers. And they weren't entirely wrong – scientists have shown that lead-based cosmetics help to prevent eye infections.

Karnak

The Temple of Karnak is the biggest religious site in the world. Building work began around 3,500 BC (before the Upper and Lower Kingdoms united) and successive rulers added to it for 17 centuries.

If you were a pharaoh, you wouldn't stop at putting your stamp on the temple at Karnak, you'd also make sure that you built a few temples in your own honour too. It was what your subjects would have wanted – although you might get them to do the actual work.

Khnum

The god Khnum was thought to create children out of clay (on a potter's wheel) and to place them in their mother's tummy.

Linen

Unwrapped, the linen bandages of an Egyptian mummy could stretch for more than two kilometres. Amulets were often wrapped in the layers of linen for good luck, although they probably had the opposite effect as the mummies then became a target for robbers in search of these valuable objects. (It was like a gory game of pass-the-parcel.)

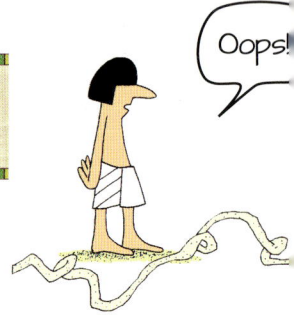

Oops!

Lighthouse

Built around 250 BC, the Pharos Lighthouse at Alexandria was one of the Seven Wonders of the Ancient World. It stood more than 120 metres tall and for many years was one of the highest man-made structures in the world (but not quite as tall as the Great Pyramid of Giza). The lighthouse, which was also a trading station, was abandoned in the 14th century after it became ruined by an earthquake.

It sure beats hitting the rocks!

Put me down quickly! I meant I needed the litter tray!

Litter

If you were of royal birth or just super important, you could get guys to carry you around on a litter (a chair carried on poles).

Mummy

Egyptians believed that to live forever you needed to preserve your body through mummification. However, it helped if your body was mummified in one piece. This was bad news for King Akhenaten's daughter. Legend says that the King was so fed up with her that, when she died, he cut off her hand so that she couldn't bother him in the Afterlife.

It wasn't just people that the Egyptians mummified. Pets were given the same honour and buried along with their owners. More than 300,000 mummified cats were discovered in a temple dedicated to Bastet, goddess of the home, and a staggering four million ibis mummies were found on the edge of Egypt's Western Desert (near Tuna el-Gebel). Perhaps the weirdest mummy was a 5.5 metre long crocodile with mummified baby crocs in its jaws.

Uh oh!

The word mummy comes from the Arabic word "mummiya", which means "tar". When the Arabs first discovered mummies, they thought they were covered in tar. However, in most cases it wasn't tar, but a dark resin, which blackened the skin.

Medicine

Egyptian doctors understood the workings of the human body. They healed many injuries and used mouldy foods or soil to treat infections (an early form of antibiotics). They even performed brain surgery – ouch!

Some Egyptian remedies were less scientific. A popular "cure" for blindness was to mash a pig's eye, mix it with red ochre and pour it into the patient's ear. A bag of mouse bones, worn round the neck, cured bed-wetting. If you think that these remedies are a bit crazy, back in England 3,000 years later, King Charles II was applying mummy dust to his skin, believing that he would absorb some of the dead pharaoh's majesty.

I thought this was a spa!

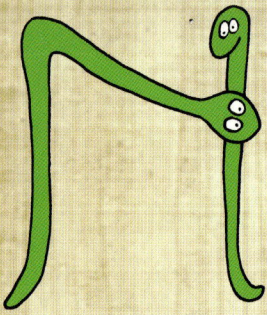

Nile

The Nile is the world's longest river, at 4,000 miles from source to sea. Every year, when it flooded, it literally "dished the dirt" and deposited rich, black soil (silt), which made the surrounding area fertile. It's no wonder that Egypt is known as the "gift of the Nile" – a phrase coined by Greek historian Herodotus 2,400 years ago.

There was nothing more important to Ancient Egyptians than the Nile. It provided food (fish and other wildlife), fresh drinking water, materials for building and clothes, transportation, and even paper (papyrus). Without the Nile, Egypt would be one humongous desert ...

Crocodiles don't sweat. They perspire!

... And without Sobek there would be no Nile. Egyptians thought that the sweat of this crocodile-headed god formed its waters.

Although the silt hung around, the water didn't. So how did Egyptians grow food in a place where it hardly ever rained? They used a shadoof (a contraption a bit like a see-saw) to scoop up water and pour it into specially dug canals and irrigation ditches to water their crops.

Osiris

Osiris was the god of the harvest and carried a shepherd's crook and flail. He ruled Egypt before being murdered by his brother, who chopped him into pieces and scattered him across Egypt. His wife, Isis, gathered up all his bits (except for one, which she replaced with gold!) and wrapped him up in bandages. He became the first mummy and, as he could no longer rule Egypt (being dead), he became King of the Underworld.

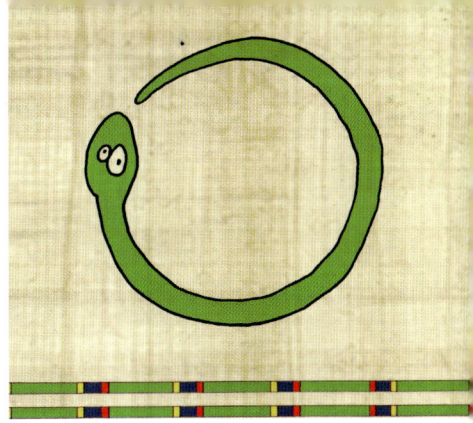

Obelisk

Pharaohs kept themselves busy by building things, such as temples, palaces and obelisks. Obelisks were tall pillars (some as high as 25 metres) and built from a single stone. They were put up in pairs in public places, such as temples. Usually, the hieroglyphics on obelisks told of battles won and other great deeds.

Several obelisks have since been transported around the world and are on display in London, New York and Rome, as well as, of course, in Egypt.

Hey! That's plagiarism.

Oar

The Nile was the easiest way to transport things and Egyptian boats were powered by wind and by oar – the largest having up to 500 rowers. One important job (the coxswain) was to shout, or sing, so that the rowers would all move in time as they rowed "merrily" down the river.

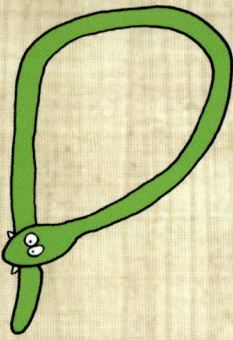

Pharaoh

Egyptians called their king "pharaoh". The word began as a nickname and meant "great house" because everyone believed the king's human body was home to a god. Before the nickname caught on, early rulers had just been called "kings". They not only had big houses, but also built themselves big tombs called pyramids.

On their death, pharaohs were shown carrying a shepherd's crook and flail – a symbol of their connection to the god Osiris.

Hatshepsut was the only queen to call herself "pharaoh". She even dressed like a man and wore a false beard.

Papyrus

Long before computers, the internet or television, the Egyptians invented a type of paper called papyrus on which to record news and events. This was made by stripping off thin slices of the papyrus reed, which grew on the banks of the Nile, and weaving them together.

There's something strange about this guy!

... two million two hundred and ninety-nine thousand nine hundred and ninety-nine ...

Pyramids

The first pyramids were built more than 4,600 years ago and were "stepped". As the Egyptians experimented with new designs, the more familiar pyramid with flat, smooth sides became the fashion.

More than 100 pyramids have been discovered in Egypt, but the most famous (and hardest to miss) is the Great Pyramid of Giza, which was one of the Seven Wonders of the Ancient World. Built as a burial place for King Khufu (or Cheops), who died in 2566 BC, it is made up of 2,300,000 stone blocks, each one weighing as much as two and a half elephants. Originally standing at 147 metres tall, the Great Pyramid at Giza remained the tallest structure in the world for 44 centuries (until the Eiffel Tower was built in 1889). Its base covers 13 acres – unlucky for those lifting the stones!

Pyramids contained great treasures buried deep inside and had a maze of secret passageways and traps to stop robbers finding them and taking them away. However, the pyramids themselves were far too easy to spot (duh!) and so later pharaohs were buried in tombs underground or in hillsides.

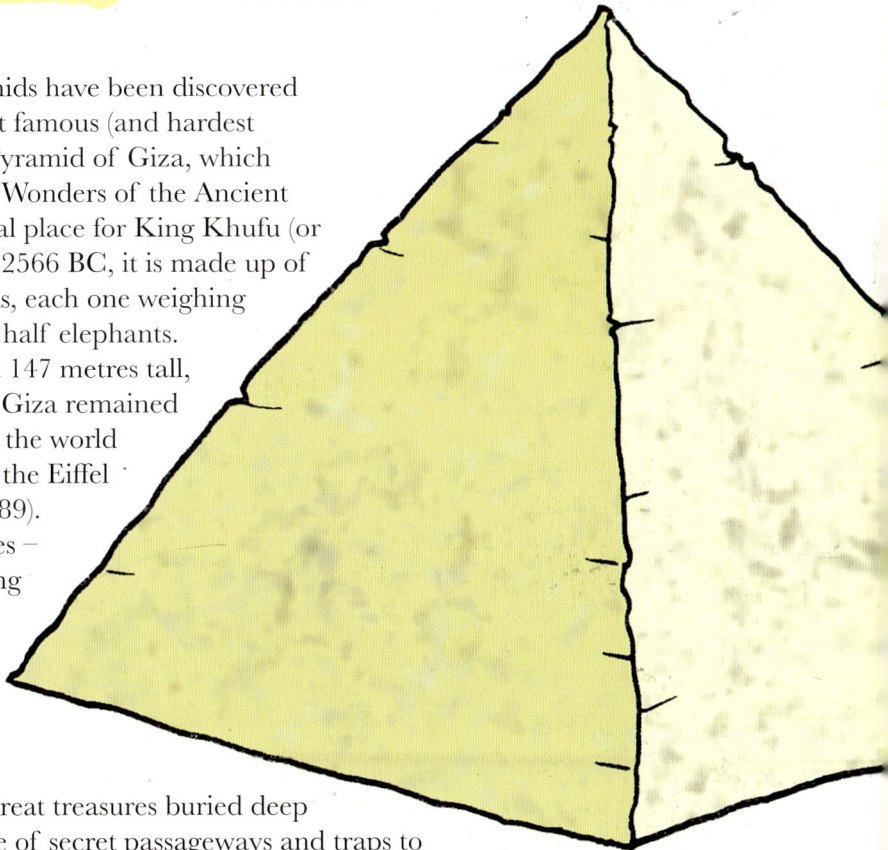

Queen of Egypt

The queen didn't have a cool name like "pharaoh"; she was just called "queen". She had important jobs such as entertaining special guests, having royal babies and looking after the pharaoh. Only a few queens ruled Egypt, for example Hatshepsut, Nefertiti and, most famous of all, Cleopatra VII, who was the last active ruler of Ancient Egypt.

Hey! Who ordered all the shrimp?

Menu

I am so beautiful!

Cleopatra VII was a member of the Ptolemic Dynasty, which was Greek. Ptolemy and his male descendants (all called Ptolemy) had ruled Egypt since the death of Alexander the Great. Cleopatra was wife to the much younger Ptolemy XIV and mother to the 15th, and final, Ptolemy. Her beauty captured the hearts of Roman leaders Julius Caesar and Marc Antony. After Antony's suicide, she killed herself with an asp – a venomous snake.

Ramesses the Great

Ramesses II (1279–1213 BC) is often considered the greatest pharaoh of Ancient Egypt.

He ruled for 67 years. He was a great soldier, a great builder and had a great number of wives. He also needed a great memory to remember the names of his 100 children.

I hate pocket-money day ...

Ramesses had red hair and a hooked nose. We know this because in 1881 his body was found in a secret chamber cut out of rock in the Valley of the Kings. To keep Ramesses' nose from collapsing, embalmers had stuffed it with peppercorns – atishoo!

Sorry, I meant the other way!

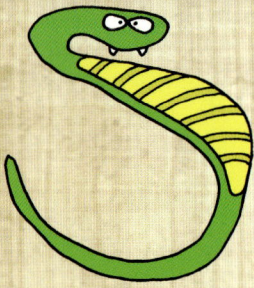

Sarcophagus

If you were royal or just pretty well off, you got more than an unceremonious burial in the sand. Once you were turned into a mummy, you got a really cool coffin, called a sarcophagus, which looked like you (sort of). Some were painted; others were covered in gold – those were the ones the tomb robbers were looking for …

NEW and USED

Sphinx

The Giant Sphinx, which guards the Great Pyramid of Giza, is one of the world's oldest monuments. It is also one of the largest. Carved out of limestone on the desert floor about 4,500 years ago, it has the body of a lion and the head of a pharaoh.

After a thousand years or so, the Sphinx became covered in desert sand. A stone tablet in front of the Sphinx tells of a young prince named Thutmose, who fell asleep near the head of the half-buried monument. He was told in a dream that, if he dug out the Sphinx, he would become a great ruler of Egypt. Thutmose got out his spade and later became pharaoh.

Snakes

Let's face it, there were a LOT of snakes in Ancient Egypt. A LOT.

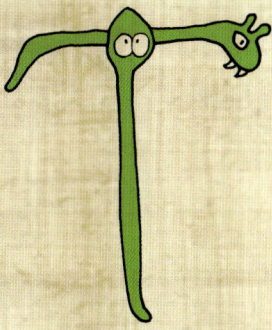

Tombs

Egyptians buried their kings, priests and rich folk in tombs. These contained elaborate paintings and statues, as well as lots of valuable stuff you might need in the Afterlife – clothes, jewellery, furniture, food and, most importantly, a loo!

I am so bored!

Despite the best plans to protect the riches hidden inside, some robbers did find their way through the network of hidden passages and secret chambers. There's gory evidence that some were better at breaking in than finding their way out!

Tutankhamen

Egyptian tombs are famous for two things – the great treasures that are buried within them and the nasty curses that befall anyone who tries to steal these treasures and the mummy away. The most famous "mummy's curse" story relates to the "Boy King" Tutankhamen, whose tomb was first opened in 1922 – 3,000 years after it had been sealed. Lord Carnarvon, one of the first to enter the tomb, died soon afterwards from an infected mosquito bite. Even more eerie, when King Tut's mummy was unwrapped in 1925, scientists discovered a wound on the left cheek – in the exact position of Carnarvon's insect bite! By 1929, 11 people connected with King Tut's discovery had died of unnatural causes.

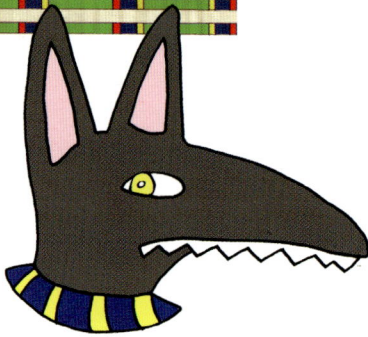

Underworld

Egyptians believed that when you died, your life force and body double (Ka) first passed into the Underworld, where the sun went at night. It was a dangerous place, where you could easily die a second time (and you thought once was bad enough). There were supernatural crocodiles, spitting snakes, boiling lakes and fierce demons to escape.

In addition, you could have your head chopped off, or you could be turned upside-down, which meant your digestive process worked in reverse, leaving a very nasty taste in your mouth! If you were lucky and well prepared, then you would reach the Afterlife – leaving the Underworld forever.

Ushabti

Even though you were dead, you still needed a few servants to get things done. Little funerary figures, called ushabti, were put in tombs to help with menial tasks in the Afterlife.

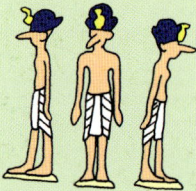

Before the Egyptians hit upon the idea of the ushabti, pharaohs buried servants with them in their tombs so they would have someone to wait on them after their death. Servants weren't buried alive, but were strangled first – how thoughtful!

Uraeus

If you were king or queen, wouldn't you want to wear a scary snake on your head? A uraeus was a symbol of royalty and divine authority.

Vizier

A vizier was an important advisor to the pharaoh – a bit like the Prime Minister. This one is making sure the pharaoh doesn't pay too much for that new chariot.

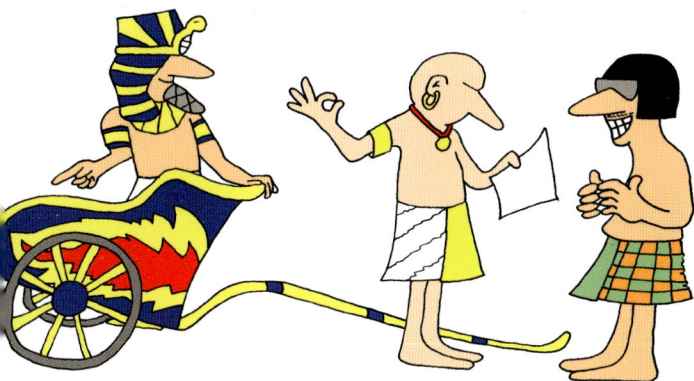

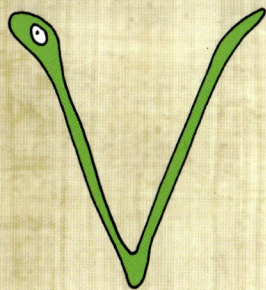

Valley of the Kings

The Valley of the Kings is a burial place on the west bank of the Nile. It was part of the ancient city of Thebes and almost all of the pharaohs in the New Kingdom (1550–1070 BC) were buried there because, well, it was new. There were no pyramids in the Valley (**so** old school). Instead, each pharaoh built a tomb with lots of corridors and chambers to house his sarcophagus. It was thought they were harder to rob. The longest tomb to be discovered belongs to Queen Hatshepsut (who pretended she was a pharaoh). Her burial chamber is almost 215 metres from the entrance to the tomb. The largest tomb was built for the sons of Ramesses II.

There are more than 60 tombs in the Valley of the Kings – archaeologists believe there are many more to discover.

You're scared?!

Wabet

The wabet was the embalming hall, where people were turned into a mummy. After drying the body in natron (like sea salt), mummies were wrapped in yards and yards of linen. The whole shebang took between 75 and 90 days.

Wigs

To stay cool and avoid lice, both men and women in Egypt shaved their heads and often wore wigs. Rich people wore wigs made from human hair, while poor people wore wigs made from wool or vegetable fibre. Women courtiers sometimes wore hair cones made of scented animal fat. When the fat melted, it made their hair smell sweet, but look greasy.

Xerxes

Although a pharaoh, Xerxes was not popular among the Egyptians. He was Persian and, having conquered Egypt in 484 BC, was too busy trying to conquer Greece to care what went on there. Instead, he left it to local governors to run the country, which in most cases meant ignoring local customs and beliefs.

> Take that, cruel sea!

Xerxes is most famous for his engineering feats. In his battles against Greece, he had two pontoon bridges built over the Dardanelles (the narrow strait dividing Europe and Asia Minor). When a storm destroyed them, Xerxes ordered the designers of the bridges to be executed and the sea to be whipped as punishment. The bridges were rebuilt and in 480 BC Xerxes, along with his army of five million (according to Heroditus), defeated the Greeks at Thermopylae.

eXtract

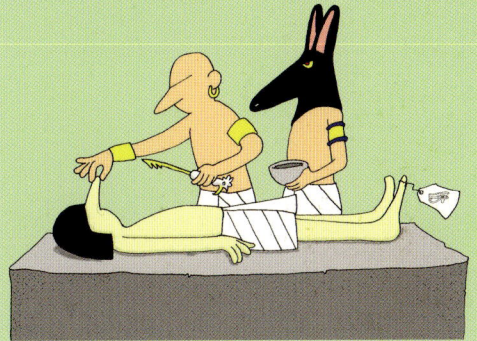

When making a mummy, Egyptians scooped out the icky stuff, some of which they saved in special canopic jars like the ones below. They saved the liver, lungs, stomach and intestines. They left the heart, which they considered to be the seat of the soul, but scooped out the brain through one of the nostrils and threw it away.

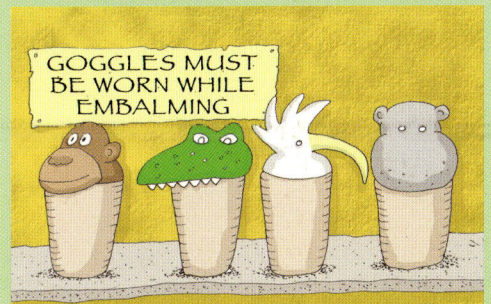

GOGGLES MUST BE WORN WHILE EMBALMING

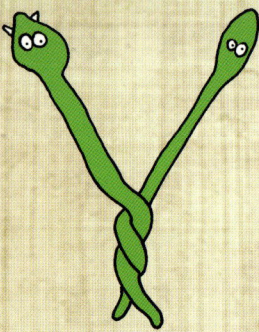

Cheers!

Year

Egyptians had three different calendars: an everyday farming calendar, an astronomical calendar and a lunar calendar. The 365-day farming calendar was made up of three seasons (flood season, planting season and harvesting season). Each season lasted four months.

The astronomical calendar was based on observations of the star Sirius, which reappeared each year at the start of the flood season.

Finally, priests kept a lunar calendar, which told them when to perform ceremonies for the moon god Khonsu.

Egyptians were the first to make raised bread using yeast. Yeast was also a vital ingredient in beer – their favourite drink.

Yummy mummy

My wedding anniversary!

Tea (made from ground-up mummy) was used to treat a variety of illnesses in Europe between the 12th and 17th centuries. Fancy a cuppa?

Zodiac of Dendera

During Napoleon's Egyptian campaign (1798–1801), the French not only discovered the Rosetta Stone, which unlocked the secret of hieroglyphics, but also the Zodiac of Dendera – a huge map of the sky. It was carved in sandstone and set into the ceiling of a small chapel in the Temple of Hathor at Dendera, near Thebes.

The map shows the constellations and the five planets known to the Ancient Egyptians. It also shows the earliest known representation of the 12 signs of the zodiac.

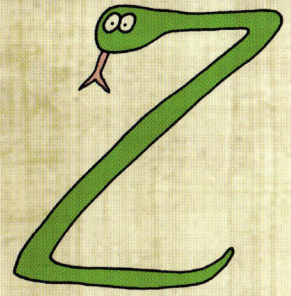

You are going on a long journey!

The Zodiac weighs three tonnes and was blasted with gunpowder from its stone surrounds by a French treasure hunter in 1821. It was then dragged for 16 days to the Nile and loaded onto a boat for France. It is now displayed in the Louvre Museum in Paris.

Based on the position of the stars, astronomers have worked out that the Zodiac of Dendera dates from about 50 BC, when Cleopatra started her reign. Cleopatra was the last ruler of Ancient Egypt – a civilisation which spanned more than 3,000 years – perhaps its ending was written in the stars!

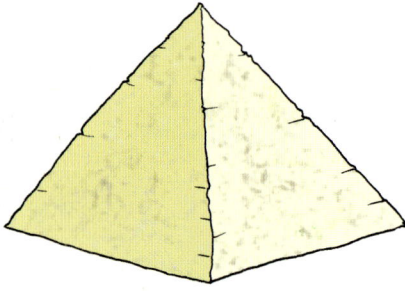

Great Pyramid (Giza)

Ramesses II

First hieroglyphics

Great Sphinx (Giza)

Tutankhamen

First written papyrus

Thutmose I

3500 BC   3000 BC   2500 BC   2000 BC   1500 BC   1000 BC

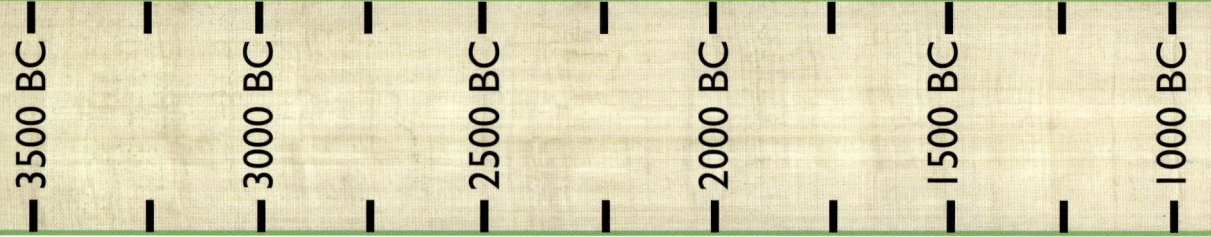

Stonehenge (England)

Lighthouse (Alexandria)

Xerxes

Egypt falls to Rome

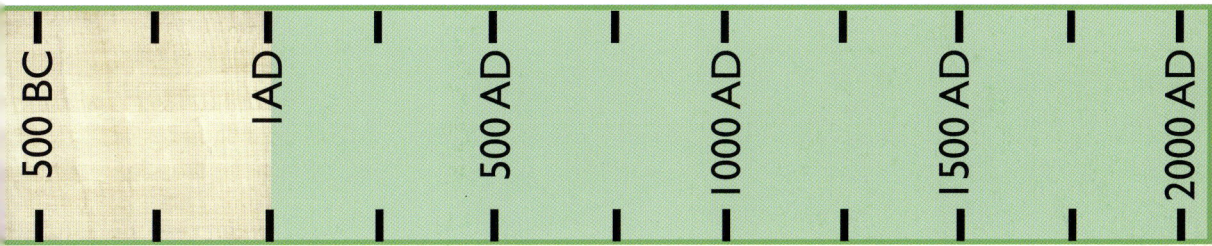

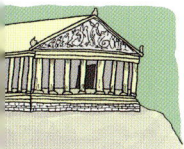

Egyptian timeline

Our timeline starts with the first hieroglyphics in about 3,250 BC – shortly before the unification of the Upper and Lower Kingdoms by King Menes, who was the first pharaoh and ruler of the whole of Egypt at around 3,000 BC.

It is more than 2,000 years since Cleopatra was Queen of Egypt and its last ruler. While this might seem a long time ago to us, for Cleopatra it would be comparatively recent – by the time she was born, the oldest pyramids would have been more than 2,500 years old.

500 BC | 1 AD | 500 AD | 1000 AD | 1500 AD | 2000 AD

Parthenon (Athens)

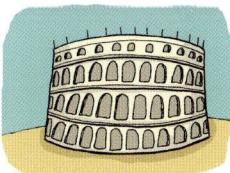

Colosseum (Rome)

Westminster Abbey (England)

Eiffel Tower (Paris)